MW00465613

Grow Older with Peers,

where laughter is contagious.

by Ruth S. Shirley

In memory of our beloved daughter,

Carrie Diane Shirley Zietz.

January 20, 1954 – February 25, 2012

Table of Contents

FORWARD

These hopefully amusing musings are not to be taken seriously. If I have offended anyone, anywhere, animal, vegetable, or mineral, living or dead it is unintentional and the people or places are all figments of my imagination.

I realize that I am not the typical senior, but neither is anyone else. I have been blessed with good health, and the very best husband, family and friends. I now have the good fortune to live in a premier, unsurpassed retirement community, and my hope is to entertain the reader with some of the lighter side of aging. We see and hear entirely too much about the darker side. Actually that is not true of this community. If ever there was an upbeat community this is it, and I hope to convey some of that spirit in my attempt to mirror it (with these figments of my imagination, of course) in these vignettes.

The reader might be interested to know that I was born on Halloween 1926, and just started this writing bit this spring and summer of 2012. You do the math, it indicates that I'm sort of the Grandma Moses of humor writing.

Our continuing care community has independent living villas (houses), and apartments; assisted living apartments; rehabilitation & skilled nursing; and memory care units in the same compound. The monthly fee for the independent living units includes long term care type insurance that enables the residents to move into the other units, when necessary, with only moderate additional costs for a few of the meals.

CHAPTER ONE

Continuing care community Resident

I'm now living in a continuing care community, which has solved a lot of problems for me. I no longer wonder, "Am I losing my memory?" Of course I'm losing my memory! Just look around me, EVERYONE is losing their memory! I, and all my new best friends whose names we can't remember, can barely find our way to the right dining room, on the right day, and at the approximate right time. We're wandering around the halls happy as larks that we're recognizing people, hoping we can read their nametags. We are just happy to be here, waking up in the morning and all. We're ecstatic that no one else can remember zilch, complete a sentence, recall a word, find their glasses, make it to the bathroom, change TV channels with their cell phone, etc., etc. We're just having fun, like a cross between college days with no exams and a cruising vacation.

Another problem that has gone by the wayside: "Where should we invest our money?" What money? That's certainly no longer a problem.

Next problem: "What will I do to fill my time?" Now that most of our chores are done for us here in our village, I should have all the time in the world to do the fun adventures, travel, hobbies, etc. that I've been putting off until just the right moment. However, while this community presents me with more and more options to keep me busy, the days seem to be getting shorter and shorter. Ye god's, how do they think up all of these activities for us to do! I couldn't participate in half of them if I were triplets. Filling in our time is no longer a problem if it ever was.

Great! The above and many other problems solved.

Too bad, though, new problems take their place – like, how do I keep the staff from noticing that I'm bonkers? Even though there's safety in numbers I don't want to be the one singled out of the herd. I try to look alert and possibly intelligent, no matter how much effort is required, and I try to remember not to do anything that will attract undue attention, since someone might be pointing a camera in my direction. Which brings up the question: "What is the problem with today's cameras?" I am a stunning blonde, with a great figure and posture, but photos make me look like a wrinkled old woman, muffin topped and hunched over, with wild hair of undetermined color! How is that possible?

Another new problem: I've downsized and this new home is smaller than my last one, how is it that there are so many more hiding places? I put lists and important items in a safe place, where I'll always remember to look first, yet when I need those lists and items they are nowhere to be found. I get most of my exercise by looking in every conceivable place, over and over, for my lost items. In the end, days later after I've reached a state of exhaustion and am now looking for something else, the lost item will be in the first place (which is now the last place) that I looked. Are there poltergeists here?

Another fascinating thing: how is it possible that I packed and brought with me everything that I'll never ever need, and left behind all the good stuff that would have been such a help. I know that I did not do this deliberately, did this happen to anyone else?

Another ongoing problem: how can I sleep in, read and loaf all day and still appear to be active and involved in all of the activities? I'm still working on that one.

DISCLAIMER

Gee, I can't remember if I told the reader that:

The preceding paragraphs were not meant to offend anyone, but are just attempts to poke fun at myself and my surroundings. I certainly did not mean to suggest that I or anyone in our community is forgetful or has "senior moments". Nor did I intend to imply that living in a continuing care community is costly, resulting in lack of money to invest. Also, I don't think members of the staff are spying on us as they are too busy thinking up more activities.

Additionally, I am well aware that my photos look just like me and I shouldn't have tried to discredit the photographers.

Pertaining to the move itself:

Don't think for a minute that we just woke up one morning and thought that it would be great fun, and sheer pleasure to work our behinds off packing, selling our house, and moving away from a home and property that we love and worked on for years to make just like we want it; then to work just as hard moving in, unpacking, and arranging (hiding) our belongings at the strange new place.

No, it has been a gradual thing, with our slowing down a little more every year. What the heck happened? Getting old was always far off on the horizon and involving someone else. Even though we certainly aren't old, 83 and 86, the fact is that we might wait too long and not be able to either make a move or stay in place, resulting in a hopeless situation.

We start looking at continuing care communities on the internet, and in person. Admittedly they are not cheap, and they are priced pretty much in line with each other, plus they seem to be filled with old people. However, when we check all of our expenses for staying in place, even if that were an option, the all inclusive expenses at the communities are not that much more.

We take the plunge, and make the move October 1, 2010. And you know what, these are not old folks living here, they are just like us. We're not old, we're just well seasoned. The smarter ones made the move sooner, so they have enjoyed it longer. The rest of us are just glad that we didn't wait any longer. We're taking charge of our future and not just leaving it to chance.

CHAPTER TWO

Some of the Joys in the Golden Years

Adult children who would be upset if Mom or Dad started showing interest in the opposite sex should keep them at home and guarded and pretend it's for their own good; and never entertain the notion of letting them loose in such a tempting environment as a continuing care community, because:

One of the joys of living in a continuing care community is seeing the romantic attachments that are made. It may come as a surprise that the elderly in their 70's, 80's and 90's are still in the game when it comes to romance, but believe me that is the case, as we are not dead yet. What a pleasure it is to see the eyes light up on a grieving, or lonely person when a new object of affection comes into view, with a matching gleam in their eye. It doesn't matter if one or both of the couple walks with a walker or is occupying a wheelchair, because in a continuing care community the more able person is not going to become the total caregiver of the other, but just the supporting companion.

Think about it. A resident has the opportunity to get to really know another person in circumstances unlike any others. Their living in the same community exposes their likes and dislikes, their taste in entertainment, their daily habits, how they treat and are treated by their children, how they present themselves in their everyday lives. Actually it's like no other situation except maybe college, which was a temporary time with personalities still being formed. Believe me the personalities of seniors are fully formed and you might even say we are set in our ways. The residents have the very best opportunity to actually get to know each other.

Then the "courtship" can be as simple as sitting together at meals, enjoying the entertainment together, attending the movies at the facility, participating in the multitude of activities, joining the various clubs, going on the fun trips, visiting in the lounges, then retreating to the privacy of their apartments. Not all of the ventures will turn into permanent attachments, after all they might discover that the other person is a Democrat or Republican or worse, but they can still be close friends and enjoy each other's company.

I'd love to see the statistics of marriages, cohabitating, or strong attachments to significant others in continuing care communities, which I'm thinking would surprise most people. I'm hoping some of my readers, if I have any, will become intrigued enough to do the research, publish a scholarly tome, and make millions. I'd prefer to be just the catalyst, since I haven't the slightest idea how to start getting the data, but I'd be more than happy to share the millions.

CHAPTER THREE

More Joys of the Golden Years

It's hard to stay lonely in a place like this with so many potential new friends. We've all made it to an advanced age and don't think that 10, 20, or 30 years separate us very much as we all have more in common than not. For instance none of us will die young, and we all have experienced a lot of the history that we wish that the children of today would study.

Furthermore new friendships are also sheer pleasure. The new friends have all led such interesting lives and it's a joy to hear about them. I have hopes that perhaps my stories that my children heard, from their birth 'til now, aren't as utterly boring as I'd begun to think and my new audience might even find them entertaining if I don't repeat them too often.

Another bonus is that maybe I'll be able to hide my worst faults and might even come nearer to becoming the person that I had aspired to be. Here's my chance, maybe my last, at trying to be my best. Hey, I'm only 85 years old, at least from now to October 31, 2012 when with luck I'll turn 86.

Before moving to a retirement community, I, the new resident should be willing to check envy at the door. The new people I meet will have traveled the world, assisted Mother Theresa, cured the ill, educated the masses, achieved multiple advanced degrees, built empires, split the atom, been rocket scientists, walked on the moon, be accomplished musicians, be renowned photographers, be the oldest living something or another, and goodness knows what other marvels, while raising a family, with their arms tied behind their backs, etc. They surely will not look down on a mere housewife but will consider my accomplishments to be amazing as well, so I'll just enjoy their triumphs along with mine. We are definitely all survivors in the same boat (make that cruise ship), and it shows in our faces and actions. Still, I do wonder what happened to all of the other housewives, did they die or what?

Bear in mind that the accomplishments of my new friends, however mind boggling , will pale in comparison to those of their grandchildren and great grandchildren, who are absolutely incredible from birth and get more amazing with every breath, and I can vouch are positively adorable because I've seen some of them.

However, don't tell a soul, my grandchildren will excel over theirs in every case, but I must try to remain modest and not brag too much to anyone.

CHAPTER FOUR

Senior Style and Fashion Guru

As I've grown older, and older, and older it has become apparent that my style and grooming choices have evolved in a fairly dramatic way and that my readers would love to benefit from my great wisdom and experience.

First I'd like to address the time factor. In my past I would shower, dress, do my hair, and put on makeup in 10 to 15 minutes. Now that preparation takes approximately all day, which means that I have had to initiate some short cuts. Some actions cannot be shortened. The shower and teeth cleaning takes 15 minutes followed by a 30 minute break. Dressing, if I laid the clothes out the night before, takes 15 minutes; so an hour has to be allotted, followed by another 15 minutes because the clothes I selected will be too tight. The time required to apply makeup can definitely be shortened since it doesn't do any good anyway. However, I do have a few rules:

1. My eyebrows should be darker than the dark circles under my eyes.

2. I must apply balm to my lips so they don't peel off and disappear entirely.

3. I should appear to be alive.

This makeup application should only take the same 5 minutes that makeup experts say would be enough time to apply astringent, moisture, foundation, false eyelashes, eyebrow pencil, mascara, eyelid stuff, blush, lip liner, lip stick with a brush, powder, and finishing spray.

My hair is cut very short and only needs finger combing and spraying, or else it will stick to my head like a swim cap, to look as good as the wild hairdos shown in today's magazines, of course the models are a good bit younger. When I wear it longer I try for more of a wind tunnel, sheep dog, or electric shock style, which also look great on the young models. Somehow, I don't know why, I never quite carry off the look like they do. Meanwhile all of the other residents seem to have manageable, glossy hair with plenty of body that looks great even after they've been in the swimming pool but I'll say no more, because as I wrote earlier, I'm supposed to have left envy at the door.

Now, moving along toward getting dressed. If I desire to wear earrings I need to allow 15 minutes to be on the safe side. There's the putting on of my glasses, the finding the earrings, the dropping of the earring back, and the searching for a flashlight to find the dropped earring back. Next there's the locating of the hole in my ear, the attempting to put the earring back on the earring sideways, and so on, but generally I eventually get them on. I would wear clip-on earrings if there was a painless way to sever the nerves to my earlobes so the clip-on type would not torture me unnecessarily.

If I want to also wear a necklace that will not slip over my head, I need to allow another 10 minutes and have at least one other person in the room with me, or I have to become a contortionist plus suffer with cramped fingers on both hands for a week. All necklace clasps are impossible to fasten except for the easily fastened magnetic ones, which inevitably are too weak and break loose allowing the necklace to fall off. This could involve losing the necklace, but that only happens if the necklace has sentimental or monetary value.

My overall dressing time has been cut to 1 hr 45 min, so I'd better allow 2 hrs in order to catch my breath.

I'm thankful that I've kept my purses, which date from the Carter administration, they look darn good and hold my stuff the same as the ones today shown for thousands, or is it millions of dollars. Saving all that money means that I have some left to carry in the purse.

Seniors are not meant to wear today's new shoes at all. I can hardly afford to look at them, and I can certainly forget about walking in them; unless I become unusually adept at walking with my heels hanging from stilts. I don't think I could even sit in the new shoes, so I take extra good care of my shoes and you should too. Mine may have to last a very long time, as I'll probably live past a hundred

& ten, and apparently they will never start making sensible shoes with reasonable heels in my size again. On the plus side, exercise shoes can be worn anywhere, with anything if you are over 55, with or without one or two pairs of socks.

Selecting what to wear from my closet is sometimes thought provoking. Will I be mingling with my peers and need a coordinating outfit that I would wear in public with my family or some of my old friends if they were living? That would be clothing I selected that wouldn't embarrass, or blind any of us and might even elicit a compliment. Or will I be with a younger crowd and need to make my selection from my recycle bin and pick plaid slacks or mini skirt with a contrasting, midriff-baring, flowered top over a longer tee shirt, a third contrast striped scarf, a floppy hat and army boots to try to impress them? Just kidding, it wouldn't matter, they'd still think I was out of it and hopefully I would be.

My newer purchases, also known as vintage clothing, are either right in style and always have been or are about to be, is the way that I look at it. This is a real boon because the latest styles are designed for 6 ft tall, size 0 streetwalkers and circus performers, plus they cost big bucks. The clothes that I bought in the 70's and 80's are my style, and perfect for today. I do need to check to see if they have disintegrated beyond belief or have huge stains. Small stains look intentional so I don't let them worry me since everyone drools a little.

Size could be an issue, but lucky you if you have any maternity outfits packed away as the tops would now be the height of fashion and now we all have the right shapes for them.

If my legs magically clear up of broken blood vessels, bruises and prominent veins; or purple paisley patterned panty hose suddenly become fashionable, I might start wearing skirts, so I need to keep my collection of skirts in various sizes and shapes as I never know when I might need them.

Incidentally, if I'm going to be indoors anywhere near air conditioning such as to dinner, entertainment, the mall, someone else's house, or the movies I need to have available a fleece or down wrap that looks light weight, even if it is 105 degrees outside, or I will be miserable and turn blue.

Fortunately, I started wearing stretchy knit tops and pants years ago because I had the foresight to know that I'd need them later since, even then, I'd change sizes several times a day. I need to have separates instead of one piece outfits because one end of me or the other will balloon out independently for no reason, at any given time.

Therefore, I try to stock every item of clothing that I might need in every size just to be on the safe side. This creates a storage problem but under the bed storage, and every spare inch of all the closets and drawers helps. I understand that some of the residents store sweaters in their never used ovens, a novel idea if a little dangerous. Of course with all these storage places the problem becomes locating the items, which I don't want to talk about.

Come to think of it, I don't want to talk about sleeveless tops, shorts, or swimsuits either.

I do hope that I've been an inspiration to those of you needing expert fashion advice and that you will come to me with any problems that you hope that I might help to solve.

CHAPTER FIVE

Senior Exercise

Continuing care communities have excellent exercise classes to keep us seniors moving about and looking alive. Unfortunately, we have to actually participate in them to receive any benefits.

But when we do attend these classes our gorgeous young instructors seem to have amnesia about us seniors obviously having done everything right up 'til now, or else we wouldn't still be here, right? They think that just because we look like blobs of putty and can hardly change positions that we must have always been couch potatoes, whereas it has only been for the last 15 or 20 years. I could tell them a thing or two, but I can't catch my breath long enough to say anything.

The first hurdle I have is trying to pick the easiest classes, yet the ones that will work the greatest miracles in the shortest time. From the descriptions on the calendar they all appear to be easy.

I think to myself, what could look easier than Beginning Yoga? The instructor assumes a position that appears to be simple and gracefully holds it. In actual practice I am required to hold a miserable position for what seems like hours, but is probably only 30 minutes, glancing at the others around me and hoping that someone can't do it and is lying there prostrate, so I can follow suit. This never happens and is quite frustrating.

Perhaps Pilates classes are the easy answer, but no, they are like Yoga on steroids. Don't be fooled that some of the movements are done on the floor, they are still impossible to execute, and that word comes to mind in several contexts while I'm thrashing around attempting to appear to be doing the movement while shaking apart but trying to continue breathing. The instructor graciously says that I am doing fine and that I will improve, which makes sense inasmuch as I can hardly do worse.

Probably water aerobics are the answer, but doesn't that require appearing in public in a swimsuit? Maybe I'll graduate to that when I mature a little.

Now Zumba classes are fun, if exhausting, but I only attend them about twice a month and each time is like starting over. I don't build up the required stamina, which would probably require daily participation and that is too tiring just to write about. The fun part of the Zumba class is that I feel like I'm carefree and dancing at the time, yet don't have to suffer the consequences until I get home and flop on the couch.

Chair aerobics, now that sounds really, really easy. It just doesn't seem possible that basically sitting in a chair can be too strenuous. Har, har. The sadistic instructor is onto that ploy, and sees to it that every muscle and bone is activated endlessly for an impossibly long time, so I can forget it. Evidently there is no easy way out.

But no, perhaps walking is the answer. I certainly know how to do that, right? While that is true, I can be certain that I'm not doing it properly. Shoulders should be pulled back and down, rib cage lifted, head up and back, and hips tucked under with the result being the posture that the experts suggest, but now I'm supposed to move forward without toppling over? Forget about it, I'll just walk like a normal human being for about 20 minutes and call it quits. Here's the scoop on that: I will not excel in that either, because the oldest resident in my community will walk circles around me and not even break a sweat. I can count on it.

Gentle stretch could certainly be my answer, but never underestimate my ability to think up excuses. Gentle stretch is held at 3 pm which I'm not up for, as it's too close to dinner and might interfere with some other activity. Besides, by that time I'm already worn out from avoiding the other classes.

You may wonder why I'm not losing weight and building muscle with all this extensive examining and checking out of the classes? It's because I haven't gone to the weight room and worked out as though I'm challenging Joe Louis to 5 rounds, that's why. In my old age it has suddenly become necessary to add weight lifting as a requirement to build muscle. In the past only Olympic contenders, boxers and wrestlers were expected to lift weights for their training. Now this poor old grandma is supposed to be in the weight room toiling away. None of that sitting in the rocking chair, enjoying myself reading novels and eating chocolates like the ladies of yore, who looked just fine thank you, is suggested.

Which reminds me, chocolate is now good for me, especially dark chocolate which I must develop a taste for. Over the decades the experts declare anything that I can think of to be first good for me, then bad for me, then good, etc. Examples: coffee good, coffee bad; running good, running bad; baby on his stomach good, baby on stomach bad; fat good, fat bad; carbohydrates good, carbohydrates bad; special vitamin good, special vitamin bad; smoking good, smoking bad; you name it good, you name it bad. Another advantage of growing old is that I can ignore the recommendations or just pick the good/bad choice that I like and go about my business.

The latest from the experts is that we're not to sit more than 3 hrs a day. What? I sit that long just eating.

There's more. Now they claim that my brain needs a workout, too. How did they determine that? They say that my brain needs all of the above physical activity plus word puzzles, taking up a new musical instrument, learning a foreign language, using my opposite hand, on and on. It's plain to see that I am in a hopeless situation.

Meanwhile the exercise experts will raise the bar continuously for the minimum time and effort that I need to expend, just to stay active, to always be just beyond my reach. This is to get them on a television program where they can show off their fit, taut, young bodies and to keep me feeling totally submissive, lazy, worn out, flabby and over the hill. I just wish that I could be around gloating when they reach my age.

The reason that I am stuck with all this thinking about exercising is that over the years I have condensed my activities to the least possible physical effort. I cut out every unnecessary job or chore in order to make living in retirement as easy and stress free as possible. Then we moved to this retirement community where I could get by doing even less. I still eat as though I have to pick cotton and plow fields and this along with my inaction is adding up. Probably what has saved me from obesity, so far, is the involuntary exercise I get from retracing my steps after entering a room and being baffled as to why I went there. I also use plenty of energy running around looking for lost objects. I should do a $200,000 study and determine that I should exercise more and eat less.

CHAPTER SIX

Senior in the Digital Age

What can I say that hasn't already been said about being jet propelled into the Digital Age as a senior without a clue? Here I am, stuck, with my brain still operating from a Card File where many of the cards are mildewed together and just occasionally flip apart on their own agenda. I'm sometimes startled when I suddenly remember, a couple of days later, something that's been nagging me. That is just my brain's Card File coming unglued and popping open on its own schedule. So I think I've partly figured out how my brain's Card File works, although I have absolutely no control over it.

Now along comes the expectation that I'm to convert my brain to electronic mode. What a seemingly impossible challenge. Sometimes I'll partially get it, for instance I'm typing this on a computer, but I never understand what I'm doing. I have many, many photos and documents stored many unknown different places in the computer somewhere. Finding those photos and documents takes entirely too much time, so that even if I'm lucky enough to locate one I can't retrace the steps I took getting there. If I write down the steps, I can't find the note, if I find the note I can't understand what I wrote.

Oh well. I did the very most important thing that I could possibly have done to operate in this new age, and that was to produce children and especially have grandchildren who do understand what's going on. They are able to direct me out of most of my disasters. Hopefully, you know some children who can help you too and we can leave it at that.

Meanwhile, surely no one likes the new phone answering system with no humans in hearing range, with their Press 1 if it's this, Press 2 if it's that, Press 3 if it's the other, Press 4 if I'd like to jump through the phone and throttle the robot, Press 5 if I've forgotten why I dialed. I know where a lot of new jobs could be created, and that's with human employees answering the phone "how may I help you".

Speaking of phones, even my fellow seniors are mastering the "smart phones" which are really computer/TV/camera/typewriter small devices that boggle my mind. They're somehow taking pictures and sending them over email or something with their phone and can show them off right away. I'm going to have to go into hiding.

In fact I'm embarrassed at how few of the features I can use on my almost primitive, simple cell phone. The one thing I do keep trying to make it do is control the TV, and that doesn't happen. I'm going to be like a former wagon master who was afraid to drive a car in the 20th century. Everything electronic is going to be sailing over my head so I must quit burying my head in the sand and try harder.

My advanced years are about to become a real asset, though, if I happen to live long enough! I can read and write cursive, which may become a lost art. I can just picture all of the young people gathered around me, observing me with awe at my amazing wisdom, and wondering how I can magically decipher their ancestor's letters from long ago. Ha, ha, so much for their flying to Mars, texting to Venus, and walking on air; only we 115 year olds will be able to read cursive let alone know how to open a letter or turn a page.

Already I'm prepared to make my mark for posterity by revealing what has happened to the artists who used to write the Lord's Prayer on the head of a pin. They have found employment writing instruction manuals, medical side effects, and ingredients of products which maybe no one else has noticed. It is unfortunate that I will not be the one wisely reading them to anyone, because I can't see the letters even with a magnifying glass. This becomes a problem when the Dr's office says to avoid taking this new medication with ones containing hydrophobiacarnix dioxide and no one, not even the young people can decipher the tiny printing on the sides of prescription bottles to determine if the ingredient is in there.

CHAPTER SEVEN

Containers

Actually opening the prescription may be as difficult as reading the precautions. This is best attempted after a good night's rest, on a sunny day when the stock market is up, and the national news is not too depressing. I will have asked the pharmacist to not use child proof tops but they have their own agenda and will have done as they please. I place the prescription bottle on a towel on a table top where I can get some leverage. Then I push down on the lid with all my strength and rotate the top clockwise, or is it counter clockwise? This will not accomplish anything but it will get me in battle mode and verify that it is in fact a child proof top. Next I find one of the jar openers that the kids have given me and try with it. This won't work either but will clear my conscience. I'll try both of these methods again just to be sure.

After that I will have to strain trying to remember how I opened the darned thing last time. With any luck a child or young adult will stroll by at this point and open it before I attack it with an axe. While the top is off I should find an easy cap to replace it or cover it with cling wrap and a rubber band.

Actually I might have had an altogether different problem than the child proof lid which requires an alternative solution. The bottle or jar might be one with invisible tape tucked just under the lid which no method will open until accidentally discovering it and prying it up with a sharp knife point. Then Eureka I can open it with just a twist. The biggest challenge is determining that the invisible tape is there in the first place.

Heaven help me with the permanent plastic enclosures around many of today's products. In this case I need to don protective gear, a jacket with stiff arms and sturdy gloves. I can see my object from all sides, but what implement will penetrate the plastic packaging? A screw driver won't pry open the layers, scissors are too weak, a machete too unwieldy, a box cutter too wimpy. Gardening shears do the trick, but now I must take the object out and dispose of the lethal plastic without lacerating myself on the sharp, ragged plastic edges. Who needs this? All I wanted was a small tube of lip balm and had to go through these contortions?

If I'm having something larger delivered, such as a pillow, it will come in a 4ft by 6ft heavy duty double box with a bushel of styrofoam peanuts that will have crumbled and become magnetic. Those will remain with me for the rest of my life, clinging to my walls, floors, and clothing. Of course I should have hefted the box outside before opening it and hopefully I didn't forget that step. The pillow in the box will have arrived unbroken in its plastic bag, which I should also take outside before opening. Now, I need to have a special kind of scissors to cut the plastic bag open so I can slip the bag off of the pillow and immediately stuff that bag into another plastic bag. Then I secure the bags with a twistem and rush them to the garbage before any more styrofoam comes loose. The pillow can now be put into use.

Of course I understand that if the delivered item was breakable the opening process would have been much more difficult.

Do not fall into the trap of trying to pull apart bags of chips, or cereal bags. The force needed to separate the top will also split it down the side in an explosion that scatters the contents everywhere. Better to cut across the top and hope it is long enough to fold down and fasten with a clothes pin. Speaking of clothes pins, make that old fashioned wooden ones not the new plastic type that split after only about 10 or 15 years of use.

CHAPTER EIGHT

The maids are coming.

One of the perks of probably all continuing care communities is weekly cleaning service of your dwelling. For me that poses an immediate challenge.

Do I want our place to be seen as one of the messiest in the complex? Do I want the maids wondering how anyone can live with such clutter? Of course not, so now we must go into combat mode the day before they are scheduled to arrive. How mortifying if they can't run the vacuum because of newspapers, magazines, and catalogues on the floor, or if they can't dust for the endlessly accumulating paperwork on all the horizontal surfaces. This escalates then into our emptying all of the trash baskets, what if they thought we generated trash? Clearing the kitchen counters and sink, what if they thought we ate and drank, sometimes cooked and dirtied dishes, glasses and utensils? Luckily we can't vacuum because we parted with the vacuum cleaner. Naturally we clear the bathroom counters of all clutter and rinse the sinks to erase any evidence that we brush our teeth or wash our faces. We think actually cleaning the bathrooms is going too far, but we do squeegee the shower because we don't want to encourage mildew.

The next hurdle is to appear to be nonchalant about it and act as though we always live this way, while also trying to become invisible while they are here.

How did we become so inundated with paper products? Our retirement village generates way more than their share, but the biggest culprits, by far, are the catalogue companies. We are on the mailing list of all catalogue companies and they are totally confused about whether we are billionaires or skinflints, so they just mail all of their publications at their reduced rate, sometimes 2 at a time, accounting for about 3-5 lbs of catalogues a day. Also all charities, politicians and past presidents think we are anxious to donate to them as soon as possible and on a continuous basis, so they paper the planet with solicitations. Credit card companies think we need dozens of cards and also assume that I want personalized checks in my name to be available to anyone aspiring to be a counterfeiter. Still, if there is nothing in our mailbox we feel neglected so it's a big tradeoff.

CHAPTER NINE

Activities

Do not fret that there will not be enough activities. I find the major problem to be that the days here are only 24 hrs long, they need to be lengthened to at least 36 hrs. Since that probably is not going to happen, I must choose among the activities that are offered, which really creates a dilemma because I cannot do them all.

Special Events
In a continuing retirement community we celebrate every event or nonevent I've ever heard of and plenty that I haven't. For example: Oscar month, Wedding

month, Dr Seuss month, Hot Dog day, May day, Mother's day, Father's day, Vanilla Ice cream day, Texas Independence day, Ground Hog day, etc. You get the picture. We are expected to wear costumes with wild hats for the some of the bigger events, which turns out to be more fun than it sounds because the outfits help us to overcome some of our inhibitions and remind us of our youth. We have activities galore to commemorate any event, along with refreshments, and the ever present photographer to immortalize the occasion.

Lectures
Informative talks are offered on no end of topics by experts from both in and out of the community. If I don't already feel dumb enough, I can attend these and marvel again about how much I didn't know and maybe learn something.

Continuing Education

Those really interested in keeping their brains working take University Continuing Education NOVA classes and love them. They're gone Wednesdays from 8:15 'til 3:30. I need to hang around because I intend to do this at a later date. Meantime I'm building up stamina for the long hours involved

Volunteering

There might be even more opportunities to volunteer here than there were back in real life. The health center is right here with all of the possibilities to befriend and assist.

The wonderful honor system library needs volunteers to keep it orderly and catalogue the donated books so we can find them.

There are endless committees to join, charities to help, plants to water, dogs to walk, errands to run, spirits to lift, new residents to welcome, prospective new residents to encourage, plus causes to volunteer for that I don't have a clue about.

Bridge

There seems to always be either a duplicate, or party bridge game in progress; so I'm sure that if I ever decide to renew my bridge skills from my Bridge Club of 50 some odd years ago, that met annually on Lincoln's Birthday, I'd be welcome to join in.

Pool

Yes, we have a pool room with a pool table and cues. It's a very attractive cozy room and there are probably avid players, but I've never actually seen anyone in there.

Bingo

Of course bingo is offered. We are seniors.

Hobbies

This an activity where we display some of our treasures that we created back when we were more active, and even some current marvelous creations from ambitious residents. This gives the residents a chance to exhibit another side or two of their previous lives.

Swimming

A lot of the residents take advantage of our lovely swimming pool and spa, and all of us should. It is a refreshing salt water pool, 3 and 4ft deep. It is great for exercise classes, doing laps, and just fooling around

Exercise

A weight room and a workout room with treadmills and bicycles are patiently awaiting my visit. I know, I know, I need to exercise there, too.

Movies

We have a very nice movie theater, where we show a nice mixture of older and newer films. I do go there prepared with a warm jacket and a fleece throw. Also sensitive souls might want to take an aisle seat in order to leave if the raunchy language in today's movies burns their ears, or if they get tired of covering their eyes. Another plus is free popcorn and iced bottled water or soft drink.

Music

Often we have musicians from the University to entertain us, and various other local groups are fun to listen to, and are usually accomplished artists.

Resident talent shows are especially enjoyable. There are wonderful pianists and other musicians living amongst us that we all love to hear. You know I don't like to brag, but I am resurrecting my guitar playing with a group that gets together every Thursday morning.

There's the pianist leader who can play anything in any key, the harmonica player, the drummer, myself, and the actual guitarist, who unfortunately is not retired so can seldom join with us, who make up the group so far.

Bird Watching and Wildlife Observing
These activities are best enjoyed in early morning or evening all around the complex. The enthusiasts have recorded and photographed many species of birds and animals. They go out early and late because they have to adhere to the wildlife's schedule, not to their own inclination to sleep in.

Classes
I have gone to a couple of these already. On a rare serious note, after the loss of our beloved Daughter to cancer this February, I participated in a Grief Counseling type class that helped a little and gave me a close kinship to the other survivors. So that type of class is offered.

I also started taking an art class that really looked interesting; but I erroneously thought that I would start painting at home again, not have to take my supplies anywhere, I'd just set them up and paint away. That hasn't happened.

I joined an excellent writing class, in late spring, along with some other really talented people. That got me started writing and it appears that I don't know how to stop.

Multiple other classes are offered in computer, bridge, you name it, or you can suggest additional ones.

CHAPTER TEN

Clubs

We try to have a club for each and every interest that you or I may have, and if there's not one you might start one. I won't because there are already more clubs than I can manage to attend, and this is probably just a partial list. Just like with all of the other topics, I will have to make choices which might depend on my mood of the day, and you don't get to hear about my multiple personality theories along that line. They will be the subject for one of my next bestselling, Pulitzer Prize winning books.

Sewing, Needlework Club

The club is what the name implies, members working on all kinds of sewing, knitting, crocheting, embroidery, and hand work . I've seen some of the magnificent quilts and embroidery that have come out of the group on display at the hobby shows. The trouble is that they probably work so hard that they seldom have time to talk.

Jewelry Design Club

Not a macaroni necklace type group. Professional style jewelry is fashioned here. Some of the jewelry has been displayed at the hobby shows and it is impressive.

Poker Club

Plenty of people are interested in Poker and they meet frequently for a good time. All that I know about it is trying to keep a poker face.

Woodworking Group

I'm assuming these are mostly men, but maybe not. They have a nice, out of the way, workshop that may work as a substitute for the one that they left behind. Some of their work has been on display and were really nice carvings and models.

Art Club

Held in the activities room. They give all the encouragement anyone could want to foster any latent artistic talent. Their lovely paintings have added to the hobby shows too. Don't fall into the trap that I have, thinking that you'll just pass and paint at home, because you won't.

Walking Club

Currently meets at 6:30 am, which is not attracting a lot of participants, although there are lots of individual walkers plus dog walkers. The walk circling the complex is ¾ of a mile.

Caregiver Support Group

This group has an extra laudable purpose, and I hope they are able to help and give encouragement to each other and their families.

Writing Club

Not in existence yet, but might materialize out of nowhere.

iPad Club

It must be quite helpful to share expertise in order to get the most out of one of those mysterious devices. Good luck!

Choral Group

This popular singing group is quite active and has entertained regularly enlivening many a program. It is open to anyone who loves to sing.

Maybe you know what the next popular clubs are about, because I surely don't.

Qigong? Mah Jong? Mexican Train?
Of course I'm sure they are fabulous.

Please forgive me if I missed a group. I
want to wish you well, too.

CHAPTER ELEVEN

Attitude

Probably the most important thing we can bring with us to a community like this is a positive attitude. By gum we don't have all that much time left and we're going to enjoy it. A few of us literally awakened here, following a routine trip to a hospital and waking up here about a month later. Others surrendered their car keys to the kids and were strongly encouraged to settle here, even bodily moved here. Most of us are here by choice and deliberately picked the place.

My spouse and I have been here 2 years this coming October 2012, and we have not seen a single sourpuss anywhere around here. Everyone is cheerful and friendly. It must be hard to be grumpy, envious, or mean spirited when you have nothing to be grumpy about and with everyone around you pleasant, seeming contented and happy. Prospective residents probably think that we're paid to act as though we love the community, but it's true that we are living more comfortably and with more creature comforts than were available to kings and queens not so long ago.

Here we can age almost any way that we want. If we want to be active we have all of the choices anyone could want. If we'd prefer to do nothing, that's available too, but admittedly a little harder to manage. We can even try out new traits, for instance if we've always been shy we can try to be a little more outgoing, if we've been domineering, well, we'll still be domineering so forget that, but the opportunity is there.

That sound that we hear wafting in the hallways, public rooms, and dining rooms is laughter. Studies show that laughter is good medicine. Wow, it doesn't cost anything and we seniors can do it all of the time. We're lucky that it's not taxed. What do we decrepit seniors have to laugh about one might ask. Ourselves, is the quick true answer. If we can laugh at ourselves, then we have endless material that we add to every day and the longer we live the better. That's decades and decades of funny episodes, mishaps, embarrassing moments, narrow escapes, plus infinite happenings that weren't the least amusing at the time. After we've chuckled over our 6, 7, 8 or more decades of hilarity we might start making fun of someone else, or not.

One thing to think about in times of minor trouble is how funny it will seem in retrospect. It might even help us to endure the discomfort at the time. I'm not thinking clowns here, but viewing setbacks in a lighter vein. Most things not only are not worth worrying about in the first place, but better yet added to our humor repertoire. Keep in perspective that we are probably not going to run for political office and thereby have every flaw or mishap exposed in every media. Besides, at our age nobody cares what we do anyway except our relatives.

What I'm saying is to try to make laughing and having fun as inevitable as death and taxes.

CHAPTER TWELVE

The Staff

I'm especially impressed with the staff here, and I'm not just trying to butter them up. They are the real reason that we feel like royalty. While they don't address me as your majesty, or your ladyship, they do come as near to it as they can. They always address me as Mrs. Shirley, and I've finally quit looking behind me to see if my mother-in-law is there. More importantly they each act as though I'm their absolute favorite resident. Alert as I am, I can't help but notice that they are the same way with all my competition. Still it's a mighty nice feeling.

I've heard the new head honcho at meetings and she sounds great, but I'm waiting until I have something to gripe about to visit with her, so that may be a long wait. Perhaps I'll relent and honor her with a visit earlier.

The first contact I had here was with the sales staff. They always greet me with a hug and they are super friendly, to the point that I think that surely we would still be best buddies even if we hadn't signed the contract. Maybe someone who didn't sign up will come forward and confirm that.

The maids are great and very professional. They dust all of the horizontal surfaces, vacuum all of the carpets, mop all of the tile, wipe down the counter tops, stove tops, and appliance fronts, dust the blinds, clean the bathrooms, sweep the decks and courtyards, and offer any additional help that we may need. For instance they will put clean sheets on the bed and launder the used sheets if needed. Employees are not allowed to accept any gratuities so we try to profess our gratitude to them with every visit. They are like our personal fantasy staff which contributes to our feeling like royalty.

The wellness director is determined that we are going to stay as healthy as possible so that we'll be prepared for any emergency and therefore keeps nagging, I mean encouraging, us to take care of ourselves, eat right and keep our records up to date. How many people were that interested in my well being out in the real world?

The maintenance people are at our beck and call, and are usually prompt especially if it seems to be a serious problem. They also change AC filters, water filters, and any other filters that they can conjure up, on a regular basis. We leave a work order for them with the concierge when we need their help, such as if our golf cart goes kaput or the icemaker quits on us.

The concierges are a special species and are never unnerved no matter what the question, the circumstance, or the crisis. Always calm and controlled they are our buffer to the outside world. They always give a friendly greeting, even while answering the phone, consoling another resident, and making notes.

The dining room staff and the kitchen staff, which are somehow connected, do everything in their power to insure that our dining experience is first class. This is probably the area where we feel the most catered to and pampered. I'm including the cocktail lounge and the snack bar in this claim.

In the dining room the hostess seats us with another couple after checking if this is acceptable to both parties. This is when we get to really visit with our friends and get acquainted with new residents, and they get to decide if they'll ever sit with us again. What a joy it is to look around at all of the tables and know most of the people that you see. Usually hovering in the background are the director and manager of dining services who hope to avert any crisis and insure our dining pleasure.

The servers usually know what I and all the other residents at the nicely set, tablecloth covered table would like to drink, cater to our multiple special requests and deliver them with aplomb. They can also describe the entrée or side order with the weird name so we non gourmets can determine if we should order it. To quote a relative "It's plain to see that I'm not a *common sewer*."The servers' attention to detail with remembering whether I am the one who likes a lot of ice or two pats of butter is ultra amazing to this forgetful resident. Maybe some of the residents had this kind of daily experience, but it is new to me.

To top it all off, we move away from the table when we are through eating, and go our merry ways without either clearing the table or tipping the server. How cool is that? It is almost impossible to find anything to complain about with the food or the service. Nevertheless, we didn't get this old without being a little persnickety and unreasonable at times.

The social director and the events manager are the liveliest people that I have ever encountered. They never wind down and are therefore tiring just to be near. They are not happy until everyone in sight seems to be having a good time, or else. They are responsible for the memorable special events that have made living here such a pleasure, and they continuously brighten the hallways and dining venues with their presence, and occasional outlandish costumes. They also make sure that we get to celebrate every possible holiday that they can unearth or dream up.

The security staff enables us to feel free to traverse the grounds and hallways safely and without fear. They are also good friends and we know that we can rely on them in any crisis. They or the maintenance crew are the ones we call if we feel threatened by a snake or have foxes in our attics. We wave at them patrolling around in golf carts and chat with them in the hallways. It's nice to know they are present like our little private army.

If I've missed anyone, they can rest assured that I meant to extol their virtues and butter them up as well as the others.

CHAPTER THIRTEEN

Our home is our castle or our deluxe stateroom on a land-cruise ship.

We've already determined that we live better than long ago royalty in their drafty, unheated, non air conditioned castles. Now let's compare our homes at our "last resort" to cruise ship staterooms. We have multiple choices of villas or apartments determined only by our desires or wallets. Our smallest apartments are equal to or better than most cruise ship deluxe staterooms with balconies. Many of the larger dwellings are as spacious as cruise ship penthouses. Our homes have spacious bathrooms, ample closets, state of the art efficient kitchens that, except for the microwave and refrigerator, are probably the least used rooms in our abodes. Our residences, from the smallest to the largest, have access to all of the amenities of the community just the same as on the cruise ships. Also like the cruise ship, without leaving the building we have available all of the activities cited in Chapter Nine, and Chapter Ten. We too have a Day Spa offering massage, Hair Salon, Manicure, Pedicure, Facials, etc.

Additionally, we have access to an in house Savings and Loan and an ATM (ATV?) machine. We each have our own mailboxes. UPS and FedEx pick up packages at the front desk for delivery. Assisted living units, rehabilitation & skilled nursing care, and memory care units are right here in an attached building for our possible future use. Nobody gets seasick. I rest my case.

We don't carry any cash and just sign for meals and any other costs the same as the cruise ships. Too bad we also have to pay up later just like they do. Here at our village we each have a monthly allowance for dining. If we spend over our allowance we are billed for the extra; if we spend less than the allowance we forfeit that amount. The great sport is to try to break even. We test all sorts of schemes to try to make that happen from ordering take-home-and freeze ice cream, to take-home-open wine, to snacks from the snack bar, to inviting guests to dine, to other ingenious ploys in order to spend the whole allowance. To cut back in the other direction, and not over spend, is not half as much fun and might even involve eating less, or ordering less expensive entrees. The competition in this sport is intense but seldom mentioned.

Our version of shore excursions is to move out the front door and onto the coach. We do not need to teeter down ramps, and stairs for a hairraising transfer to a rocking Tender to get ashore. Admittedly the excursions that we take are not as exotic as those at foreign ports, but they would seem so if a cruise ship would just dock in a nearby lake.

Some of our trips are just for convenience, say to the grocery, or the Doctor, but others are for enjoyment. The coach is regularly used to take the residents to area parks for an outing, local malls, popular restaurants, local attractions and events, plus UT football games are a destination during the season. Central Texas has plenty to offer with nearby destinations such as Wimberly, Waco, Johnson City, Fredericksburg, on and on.

Sometimes we go further afield and contract with a tour bus. A trip to Branson, Missouri was a big success; and so was the cruise out of Galveston which was enjoyed by all, in spite of what I've been writing. I know the meals can't have been any better nor the staterooms more comfortable than our residences; but when cabin fever strikes, and wanderlust hits, travel is about the only remedy.

CHAPTER FOURTEEN

The Health Center

The Health Center is an amenity that we're all paying for and maybe is the real reason that we moved here. Inevitably, if we don't have the good fortune of just keeling over while in perfect health, we will be availing ourselves of the Health Center.

Still, even though I think that I'm basically a tightwad (my spouse might disagree), I'd just as soon donate that "long term care type insurance" and never need to use it. That option is not up to me, except perhaps to the extent that I take care of myself. If and when we do utilize the center, we are extremely fortunate that it is a first class facility with a staff that everyone who has even wandered into the place has praised. The volunteers, who are helping out there, are deservedly getting in points with the powers that be.

We all know that it is there for us and we hope to make use of it – just not now.

Ruth Slocum Shirley was born Ruth Margaret Hollingshead in Healdton, OK, on Halloween 1926, and later took the surname of her stepfather (when traveling all over the US with his mother and stepfather, she was called Ruth Margaret Hollingshead Slocum Patterson). She began school in Pampa, TX followed by High School in Orange, TX where she was a member of the Bengal Guards. At college she was a Delta Gamma Sorority member. Ruth was married in 1948, and graduated the next day from the University of Texas in Austin. She has thrived as a daughter, sister, wife, mother, and grandmother. She has worked in sales, as an artist, a musician, volunteer, traveler, decorator, seamstress, retiree, coach, friend, landscaper, genealogist, jack of all trades, master of a few, and now as a late blooming author.